Disclaimer

The material contained in this book is for information purpo[ses]
anyone undertaking a physical training program should con[sult]
prior to undertaking a the program. The author or anyone involved with the publication of this material cannot be held responsible for injuries caused while carrying out the program or exercises listed in the following book.

Copyright

None of the material in this publication may be copied, used or broadcast in any way without the express permission of the author. Copyright 2013 By Peter North. All Rights Reserved.

What is Combat Readiness?

Full Spectrum Special Forces Operations place a high load on an operator's physical and mental conditioning. With massive stress placed on an operator's strength, stamina, resilience and coordination. Victory-and more importantly an operators life will depend on this if he's to be operate effectively in combat situations.

Combat Readiness is defined as:

"The ability to meet the Physical and Mental demands of any active combat position, meet mission objectives, and continue to the next set of mission objectives in The shortest time possible to achieve victory"

Physical readiness training provides the **foundation for all mission specific readiness raining.** You must have in place on a personal level or have access to a "Combat Readiness Training" program at all times. It should be accessible from your direct superiors or unit commanding officers. The aim of this book is to give you a CRT plan which you will have access to at all times. Not only must you meet the basic physical standards but you must also keep your conditioning as high as possible after you complete any selection and basic training.

Train as you will fight

"Train as you will fight" is the basic principle of any combat training program. This principle should also carry over into your combat readiness conditioning.

In order to achieve the specific aims of being an effective combat readiness program certain rules must be followed as to the types of conditioning used in designing your program.

Combat Readiness Conditioning Guidelines

- Your CRT program must provide an effective foundation in order to allow for quick transition to a mission specific program.
- Your CRT must allow you to participate in varied tasks within combined arms operations.

- Must focus on training the fundamentals of operational requirements first.
- Must be performance focused, realistic and mission orientated.
- Should include challenging, complex and unusual situations.
- Must be conducted under conditions that replicate operational situational factors.
- Can be adapted for use during deployments.

Realism

This program will aim to incorporate realism in as safe a fashion possible to allow you experience something as close as possible to the pressure you will face during training or preparing for your military deployment. It will include all the fundamental skills you may use such as jumping, climbing, landing and movement with a load.

Performance-Orientated Conditioning

Performance-Orientated training means your conditioning is focused onto those skills you will most perform in your combat deployment. Each of your operational tasks and training drills is made of unique physical movements which must be conditioned in the correct way. In the table below you will find a breakdown of all of the movement's specific to different areas of combat. The tasks prodced on this chart are the result of analysis into mission loads and movement factors present during operations in many different spheres of combat deployment.

Shooting, deployment of grenades or thrown objects	-Run under load -Jump or bound -High/Low Crawl -Climbs -Push/Pull -Changes of Direction -Get up/down -Rolls -Throw
Individual movements, Movement from point A to B, Move under fire	-Run under load -Jump or bound -High/Low Crawl

	-Climbs -Push/Pull -Changes of Direction -Get up/down -Rolls -Throw -Marching -Swims -Sprints under load
Performance of Combative Techniques	-React to man to man contact -push, pull -Roll -Throw, land -Manipulate bodyweight -Rotate, bend -Block, strike, kick
Adapting to unexpected situations, assess and escalate violence	-Run under load -Jump or bound -High/Low Crawl -Climbs -Push/Pull -Changes of Direction -Get up/down -Rolls -Throw -Marching -Swims -Sprints under load -React to man to man contact -push, pull -Roll -Throw, land -Manipulate bodyweight -Rotate, bend -Block, strike, kick
Battle Drills, React to contact, Evacuate a Casualty	-Run under load -Jump or bound -High/Low Crawl -Climbs -Push/Pull

	-Changes of Direction
	-Get up/down
	-Rolls
	-Throw
	-Marching
	-Swims
	-Sprints under load
	-React to man to man contact
	-push, pull
	-Roll
	-Throw,land
	-Manipulate bodyweight
	-Rotate,bend
	-Block, strike, kick
	-load,lift or carry

In order for you to be at full operational capacity you must be conditioned in all of these situations to the full. As you can see the more violent the situation the more physical and demanding it may get making complete conditioning a must if you are perform you combat skills to maximum standard during your operational deployment. It is this concept and the above chart the make up the focus of the following operator cantered conditioning program.

The Golden Triangle of Military Conditioning

This program follows what they call an integrated approach to SOF conditioning by training what can be called the "Golden Triangle" of Military Conditioning. Based on the research discussed above and the breakdown of movements displayed in multiple operational situations there are three key areas which must be focused on:

- Endurance
- Strength
- Mobility

In order to meet the physical needs demanded based on operational needs the SOF operator must meet physical standards in all of the above areas. If operators meet these standards the will maximise their combat potential. Not only that but they will maintain this for longer both in terms operational duration and in length of operational career or term of service.

The Modern SOF Operator

During the past 10 years the operational load of SOF has hit an all time peak and looks set to continue. Operations are now conducted via a SOF network that requires 24 hour operational turn over with the next operations planned within a 24 hour time frame. This rate is then maintained for the duration of the operational rotation which can last 4-6 months. Now more than ever traditional methods of conditioning SOF soldiers are falling short of preparing soldiers for operational standards with an increasing amount of preventable injuries, operational burn outs and exhaustion being the end result. There is a strong need for not only an in depth SOF specific Strength and Conditioning framework and doctrine but also an increased need for many other factors. Injury prevention, rapid rehabilitation and correct monitoring of an Operators conditioning at an SOF specific level are also crucial. One final point not covered is educational needs of the operators themselves. It is vital SOF operators buy into and fully understand the needs and reasoning behind the new ways of approaching the physical demands of SOF performance.

Operator Focused Conditioning

The core of this program is the concept that **THE SOF OPERATIVE IS THE MOST IMPORTANT WEAPON. MAXIMISE THE MAN AND YOU MAXIMISE HIS IMPACT AS A SOF OPERATIVE.** All aspects of this program are focused with that core belief. The individual, his craft skills and intelligence in the field are the true keys to mission success. Only when the individual is fully conditioned in a manner specific to operational load demands will there be peak performance. Not only that but having a high performance SOF specific conditioning program in place under refinement on an ongoing basis is the best way to provide operator longevity. This allows operators to serve for longer in combat roles of further training positions for new operatives.

US Marine 8 Week Strength and Conditioning Program

You will complete this program by executing the following principles:

1. Workout with at least 1 day of rest between Workouts
2. Begin each workout with Core Strength

Week 1

- The objective of this phase is to learn the movements provided
- Perform 8 repetitions of each movement with 2 minutes rest between sets
- Perform 3-4 sets of each movement in the order provided
- Front Squat
- Dead Lift
- Hang Clean and Press
- Kettle Bell Swing
- Pull Up
- Power Clean
- Bench Press
- Core movements-Goblet Squat, Kettlebell Crunches, Turkish Get Up, Kettlebell Twists
- 1 Mile Run Performed 3 times per week

Week 2

- You will start with "Doubles" which is one strength move followed by a sprint
- You will use the moves learnt in week 1
- Sprints will be 20 seconds followed by 10 seconds walking back to the start point to begin again
- You will perform these sprints wearing a light weight vest of at least 10-15lb
- Perform 2 of each "Double" outlined in the workout

- Day 1-Bench Press 8 Reps + 20 Seconds Sprints, Front Squat 8 Reps + 20 Second Sprint
- Day 2- Pull Ups to Failure + 20 Seconds Sprints, Dead Lift 8 Reps + 20 Second Sprints
- Day 3-Bench Press 8 Reps + 20 Second Sprints, Front Squats 8 Reps + 20 Seconds Sprints
- 1.5 Mile Run performed 3 timed per week

Week 3

- You will progress to "Triples" which is one upper body strength move and lower body strength move followed by a sprint
- You will use the moves learnt in week 1
- Sprints will be 20 seconds all out
- Rest 60 Seconds between each Triple
- You will perform these sprints wearing a light weight vest of at least 10-15lb
- Perform 3 of each "Double" outlined in the workout
- Day 1- Front Squats 8 Reps + Bench Press 8 Reps + 20 Seconds Sprints
- Day 2- Dead Lifts 8 Reps + Pull Ups to Failure + 20 Seconds Sprints
- Day 3-Pwer Clean 8 Reps + Bench Press 8 Reps + 20 Second Sprints
- 2 Mile run performed 3 times per week

Week 4

- You will progress to "Triples" which is one upper body strength move and lower body strength move followed by a sprint
- You will use the moves learnt in week 1
- Sprints will be 20 seconds all out
- Rest 45 Seconds between each Triple
- You will perform these sprints wearing a light weight vest of at least 15-25lb
- Perform 3 of each "Double" outlined in the workout
- Day 1- Front Squats 8 Reps + Bench Press 8 Reps + 20 Seconds Sprints
- Day 2- Dead Lifts 8 Reps + Pull Ups to Failure + 20 Seconds Sprints
- Day 3-Pwer Clean 8 Reps + Bench Press 8 Reps + 20 Second Sprints

- 2.5 Mile run performed 3 times per week

Week 5

- You will progress to "Triples" which is one upper body strength move and lower body strength move followed by a sprint
- You will use the moves learnt in week 1
- Sprints will be 20 seconds all out
- Rest 30 Seconds between each Triple
- You will perform these sprints wearing a light weight vest of at least 25-35lb
- Perform 3 of each "Double" outlined in the workout
- Day 1- Front Squats 8 Reps + Bench Press 8 Reps + 20 Seconds Sprints
- Day 2- Dead Lifts 8 Reps + Pull Ups to Failure + 20 Seconds Sprints
- Day 3-Pwer Clean 8 Reps + Bench Press 8 Reps + 20 Second Sprints
- 3 Mile run performed 3 times per week

Week 6

- You will progress to "Triples" which is one upper body strength move and lower body strength move followed by a sprint
- You will use the moves learnt in week 1
- Sprints will be 20 seconds all out
- Rest 30 Seconds between each Triple
- You will perform these sprints wearing a light weight vest of at least 30-40lb
- Perform 3 of each "Double" outlined in the workout
- Day 1- Front Squats 8 Reps + Bench Press 8 Reps + 20 Seconds Sprints
- Day 2- Dead Lifts 8 Reps + Pull Ups to Failure + 20 Seconds Sprints
- Day 3-Pwer Clean 8 Reps + Bench Press 8 Reps + 20 Second Sprints
- 2x3 mile run and 1x3 mile run at best effort aim for under 20 minutes

Week 7

- You will progress to "Triples" which is one upper body strength move and lower body strength move followed by a sprint
- You will use the moves learnt in week 1
- Sprints will be 20 seconds all out
- Rest 30 Seconds between each Triple
- You will perform these sprints wearing a light weight vest of at least 40-50lb
- Perform 3 of each "Double" outlined in the workout
- Day 1- Front Squats 8 Reps + Bench Press 8 Reps + 20 Seconds Sprints
- Day 2- Dead Lifts 8 Reps + Pull Ups to Failure + 20 Seconds Sprints
- Day 3-Pwer Clean 8 Reps + Bench Press 8 Reps + 20 Second Sprints
- 2x3 mile runs aim to complete both under 20 minutes plus one 4 mile run

Week 8

- You will progress to "Triples" which is one upper body strength move and lower body strength move followed by a sprint
- You will use the moves learnt in week 1
- Sprints will be 20 seconds all out
- Rest 30 Seconds between each Triple
- You will perform these sprints wearing a light weight vest of at least 40-50lb
- Perform 3 of each "Double" outlined in the workout
- Day 1- Front Squats 8 Reps + Bench Press 8 Reps + 20 Seconds Sprints
- Day 2- Dead Lifts 8 Reps + Pull Ups to Failure + 20 Seconds Sprints
- Day 3-Pwer Clean 8 Reps + Bench Press 8 Reps + 20 Second Sprints
- 2x4 mile runs plus one 5 mile run

SBS General Physical Conditioning Test

Name_____ Date_____ Test Number=_____

3 Mile Run Under 20 minutes	Time	100 points for completing in under 20 minutes, +3 points for every 15 seconds under, -3 points for every 15 seconds over
Max Pull Ups		5 Points for ever Pull Up with good form
Max Full Sit Up 2 Minutes		1 Point Per Sit Up
Box jump -3 different size boxes 60 cm, 45 cm and 30 cm. Complete one rep jump over each from a 2 footed start in smallest to largest order then sprint back to the start. Each box should placed 1.5 meters apart in a vertical line.	Max reps in 1 Minute	10 Points per repetition
Max Press Up 1 Minute		1 Point Per repetition
Max Back Extensions 1 Minute		1 Point Per repetition
Max Burpees 1 Minute		2 Points Per repetition
Max Incline Sit Up 1 Minute		1 Point Per Repetition
Max 20 Foot Rope Climbs 1 Minute		10 Points Per Climb
Max Lateral Jumps 1 Minute		1 Point Per Jump

Average 350-500 Points
Pass 500-650 Points
Royal Marine Pass 650-750 Points
SBS 750+ Points

Week 1	
Monday	3 Mile Run best effort to be completed in 20 minutes
Tuesday	20 Minutes Swimming Boots+Trousers Rope workouts 3 climbs in rapid sped with 10lb weight vest
Wednesday	Regular Pull Ups 50 Dips 50 Push Up 100 Diamond Push Up 100 Burpees 100 Perform 100 of all exercises in sets of 25 and Pull Ups and Dips in sets of 10
Thursday	1 Hour running steady state 70 intensity at incline 2-3% if doing it on treadmill

Friday	Military Skills Circuit
	-Use an Arm, Trunk and Leg alternating set up
	-Circuit 1 Pull Ups to failure
	      Sit Ups twist
	      Squat
	-Circuit 2 Chins to failure
	      Sit Ups Twist
	      Step Ups Weighted
	-Circuit 3 Bench Press
	      Back Extensions
	      Box Jumps
	12 Repetitions each exercise perform circuit 3 times

Saturday	Rest
Sunday	2 Hours pack marching with 30lb pack

Week 2	
Monday	40 Minutes run in boots+trousers+t-shirt
Tuesday	Regular Pull Ups 75 Dips 75 Push Up 125 Diamond Push Up 125 Burpees 125 3 rope climbs fast speed 15-20lb load
Wednesday	Interval Swimming 1 Minute Sprint Swim 10 minutes Slow Swimming Repeat 4 times
Thursday	2 Hour pack march carrying 35lb pack
Friday	1 Hour pack march carrying 35lb pack at a faster pace
Saturday	Regular Pull Ups 75 Dips 75 Push Up 125 Diamond Push Up 125 Burpees 125
Sunday	Rest

Week 3	

Monday	40 Minutes running in boots+trousers 8x100 Sprints 10lb weight vest

Tuesday	Military Skills Circuit
	-Use an Arm, Trunk and Leg alternating set up
	-Circuit 1 Pull Ups to failure
	      Sit Ups twist
	      Squat
	-Circuit 2 Chins to failure
	      Sit Ups Twist
	      Step Ups Weighted
	-Circuit 3 Bench Press
	      Back Extensions
	      Box Jumps
	Increase the weight and perform 10 Repetitions each exercise perform circuit 3 times

Wednesday	Interval Swimming 1 Minute Sprint Swim 10 minutes Slow Swimming Repeat 6 times
Thursday	2 Hour pack march carrying 40 lb pack
Friday	1 Hour 30 mins pack march carrying 40lb pack at a faster pace
Saturday	Regular Pull Ups 100 Dips 100 Push Up 150 Diamond Push Up 150 Burpees 150
Sunday	Rest

Week 4	

Monday	Regular Pull Ups 100 Dips 100 Push Up 150 Diamond Push Up 150 Burpees 150
Tuesday	2 Hour pack march carrying 45lb pack
Wednesday	8 Mile best effort run
Thursday	Rest
Friday	1 Hour 30 minutes pack march carrying 45lb pack at a faster pace

Saturday	Military Skills Circuit
	-Use an Arm, Trunk and Leg alternating set up
	-Circuit 1 Pull Ups to failure
	    Sit Ups twist
	    Squat
	-Circuit 2 Chins to failure
	    Sit Ups Twist
	    Step Ups Weighted
	-Circuit 3 Bench Press
	    Back Extensions
	    Box Jumps
	Increase the weight and perform 8 Repetitions each exercise perform circuit 3 times

Sunday	50 Minutes running steady state 70 intensity at incline 2-3% if doing it on treadmill

Week 5	

Monday	3 Mile Run best effort to be completed in 20 minutes
Tuesday	25 Minutes Swimming Boots+Trousers-t-hisrt Rope climbs in 15-20lb load
Wednesday	2 Hours pack march 45lb pack

Thursday	Military Skills Circuit
	-Use an Arm, Trunk and Leg alternating set up
	-Circuit 1 Pull Ups to failure
	      Sit Ups twist
	      Squat
	-Circuit 2 Chins to failure
	      Sit Ups Twist
	      Step Ups Weighted
	-Circuit 3 Bench Press
	      Back Extensions
	      Box Jumps
	Increase the weight and perform 4-6 Repetitions each exercise perform circuit 3 times

Friday	1 Hour running steady state 70 intensity at incline 2-3% if doing it on treadmill
Saturday	Regular Pull Ups 125 Dips 175 Push Up 175 Diamond Push Up 175 Burpees 175
Sunday	2 Hours pack marching 50lb pack

Week 6	
Monday	60 Minutes running steady state 70 intensity at incline 2-3% if doing it on treadmill

Tuesday	Military Skills Circuit
	-Use an Arm, Trunk and Leg alternating set up
	-Circuit 1 Pull Ups to failure
	      Sit Ups twist
	      Squat
	-Circuit 2 Chins to failure
	      Sit Ups Twist
	      Step Ups Weighted
	-Circuit 3 Bench Press
	      Back Extensions
	      Box Jumps
	Increase the weight and perform 12 Repetitions each exercise perform circuit 3 times use 10lb weight on pull up and chins

Wednesday	12.5 Mile Endurance march 35lb pack to be completed in 3 hours 25 minutes
Thursday	Regular Pull Ups 150 Dips 150 Push Up 175 Diamond Push Up 175 Burpees 175
Friday	60 Minutes running steady state 70 intensity at incline 2-3% if doing it on treadmill
Saturday	Regular Pull Ups 150 Dips 150 Push Up 175 Diamond Push Up 175 Burpees 175
Sunday	Rest

Week 7	
Monday	50 Minutes running boots+trousers , t-shirt 4-6x150 sprints 15-20lb load

Tuesday	Military Skills Circuit
	-Use an Arm, Trunk and Leg alternating set up
	-Circuit 1 Pull Ups to failure
	      Sit Ups twist
	      Squat
	-Circuit 2 Chins to failure
	      Sit Ups Twist
	      Step Ups Weighted
	-Circuit 3 Bench Press
	      Back Extensions
	      Box Jumps
	Increase the weight and perform 10 Repetitions each exercise perform circuit 3 times 10lb load on pull ups and chins

Wednesday	Rest
Thursday	50 Minutes Interval runs to include 8x1 Min Hill Sprints
Friday	Interval Swimming 1 Minute Sprint Swim 10 minutes Slow Swimming Repeat 4 times
Saturday	Regular Pull Ups 175 Dips 175 Push Up 200 Diamond Push Up 200 Burpees 200
Sunday	Rest

Week 8	
Monday	55 Minutes Interval runs to include 8x1 Min Sprints
Tuesday	2 Hour 30 mins pack march carrying 50 lb pack
Wednesday	1 Hour pack march carrying 50 lb pack faster pace
Thursday	8 Mile run best effort
Friday	Rest

Saturday	Military Skills Circuit
	-Use an Arm, Trunk and Leg alternating set up
	-Circuit 1 Pull Ups to failure
	      Sit Ups twist
	      Squat
	-Circuit 2 Chins to failure
	      Sit Ups Twist
	      Step Ups Weighted
	-Circuit 3 Bench Press
	      Back Extensions
	      Box Jumps
	Increase the weight and perform 8 Repetitions each exercise perform circuit 3 times 15lb load on pull ups and chins

Sunday	2 Hour 30 mins pack march carrying 55 lb pack

Week 9	
Monday	3 Mile run to be completed in 20 minutes
Tuesday	35 Minutes Swimming Rope climbs with 25-50lb load
Wednesday	2 Hour 30 Mins pack march carrying 55 lb pack
Thursday	1 Hour running steady state 70 intensity at incline 2-3% if doing it on treadmill

Friday	Military Skills Circuit
	-Use an Arm, Trunk and Leg alternating set up
	-Circuit 1 Pull Ups to failure
	    Sit Ups twist
	    Squat
	-Circuit 2 Chins to failure
	    Sit Ups Twist
	    Step Ups Weighted
	-Circuit 3 Bench Press
	    Back Extensions
	    Box Jumps
	Increase the weight and perform 12 Repetitions each exercise perform circuit 3 times 15lb load on pull ups and chins

Saturday	Regular Pull Ups 200 Dips 200 Push Up 225 Diamond Push Up 225 Burpees 225
Sunday	1 Hour pack march carrying 55 lb pack faster pace

Week 10	
Monday	60 Minutes running steady state 70% intensity 2-3% incline must at least 8x1minute hill sprints
Tuesday	8 Mile endurance pack march 61lb to be completed in 1 hour 50 minutes
Wednesday	Interval Swimming 1 Minute Sprint Swim 10 minutes Slow Swimming Repeat 6 times
Thursday	60 Minutes running steady state 70% intensity 2-3% incline
Friday	Regular Pull Ups 225 Dips 225 Push Up 250 Diamond Push Up 250 Burpees 250
Saturday	Regular Pull Ups 225 Dips 225 Push Up 250 Diamond Push Up 250 Burpees 250
Sunday	3 Hour pack march carrying 61 lb pack

Week 11	
Monday	60 Minutes running steady state 70% intensity 2-3% incline must at least 10x1minute hill sprints

Tuesday	Military Skills Circuit
	-Use an Arm, Trunk and Leg alternating set up
	-Circuit 1 Pull Ups to failure
	    Sit Ups twist
	    Squat
	-Circuit 2 Chins to failure
	    Sit Ups Twist
	    Step Ups Weighted
	-Circuit 3 Bench Press
	    Back Extensions
	    Box Jumps
	Increase the weight and perform 4-6 Repetitions each exercise perform circuit 3 times

Wednesday	3 Hour pack march carrying 61 lb pack
Thursday	3 Hour pack march carrying 61 lb pack
Friday	50 Minutes continuous swimming
Saturday	Regular Pull Ups 250 Dips 250 Push Up 275 Diamond Push Up 275 Burpees 275
Sunday	60 Minutes running steady state 70% intensity 2-3% incline

Week 12	
Monday	60 Minutes running steady state 70% intensity 2-3% incline must at least 10x1minute hill sprints

Tuesday	Military Skills Circuit
	-Use an Arm, Trunk and Leg alternating set up
	-Circuit 1 Pull Ups to failure
	      Sit Ups twist
	      Squat
	-Circuit 2 Chins to failure
	      Sit Ups Twist
	      Step Ups Weighted
	-Circuit 3 Bench Press
	      Back Extensions
	      Box Jumps
	Increase the weight and perform 4-6 Repetitions each exercise perform circuit 3 times 15-20lb load on pull ups and chin

Wednesday	3 Hour pack march carrying 61lb pack
Thursday	3 Hour pack march carrying 61 lb pack
Friday	55 Minutes continuous swimming
Saturday	Regular Pull Ups 275 Dips 275 Push Up 300 Diamond Push Up 300 Burpees 30
Sunday	60 Minutes running steady state 70% intensity 2-3% incline

12 week Pre-selection Program

Monday	3 Mile Run

	Perform 3-4 sets of each movement in the order provided 12 reps per movement Front Squat Dead Lift Hang Clean and Press Kettle Bell Swing Pull Up Power Clean Bench Press
Tuesday	20 Minutes Swimming 25 Pull Ups 50 Squats 100 Press Ups 200 Sit Ups
Wednesday	Perform 3-4 sets of each movement in the order provided 12 reps per movement Front Squat Dead Lift Hang Clean and Press Kettle Bell Swing Pull Up Power Clean Bench Press
Thursday	1 Hour running steady state 70 intensity at incline 2-3% if doing it on treadmill Sprints 8x50 M 10lb weight vest 30 secs rest between sprints
Friday	Perform 3-4 sets of each movement in the order provided 12 reps per set Front Squat Dead Lift Hang Clean and Press Kettle Bell Swing Pull Up Power Clean Bench Press
Saturday	Rest
Sunday	2 Hours pack marching with 30lb pack

Week 2 Monday	3.5 Mile Run

	Perform 3-4 sets of each movement in the order provided 10 repetitions Front Squat Dead Lift Hang Clean and Press Kettle Bell Swing Pull Up Power Clean Bench Press
Tuesday	25 Minutes Swimming 35 Pull Ups 60 Squats 110 Press Ups 210 Sit Ups
Wednesday	Perform 3-4 sets of each movement in the order provided 10 reps per movement Front Squat Dead Lift Hang Clean and Press Kettle Bell Swing Pull Up Power Clean Bench Press
Thursday	1 Hour running steady state 70 intensity at incline 2-3% if doing it on treadmill Sprints 8x50 M 25lb weight vest 30 seconds rest between sprints
Friday	Perform 3-4 sets of each movement in the order provided 10 reps per set Front Squat Dead Lift Hang Clean and Press Kettle Bell Swing Pull Up Power Clean Bench Press

Saturday	Rest
Sunday	2 Hours 30 Minutes pack marching with 45lb pack

Week 3	
Monday	4 Mile Run
	Perform 3-4 sets of each movement in the order provided 8 reps per movement
	Front Squat
	Dead Lift
	Hang Clean and Press
	Kettle Bell Swing
	Pull Up
	Power Clean
	Bench Press
Tuesday	30 Minutes Swimming
	40 Pull Ups
	65 Squats
	120 Press Ups
	215 Sit Ups
Wednesday	Perform 3-4 sets of each movement in the order provided 8 reps per movement
	Front Squat
	Dead Lift
	Hang Clean and Press
	Kettle Bell Swing
	Pull Up
	Power Clean
	Bench Press
Thursday	1 Hour running steady state 70 intensity at incline 2-3% if doing it on treadmill

	Sprints 4-6x100 M 25lb weight vest 30 seconds rest between sprints
Friday	Perform 3-4 sets of each movement in the order provided 8 reps per set Front Squat Dead Lift Hang Clean and Press Kettle Bell Swing Pull Up Power Clean Bench Press
Saturday	Rest
Sunday	2 Hours 30 Minutes pack marching with 55lb pack

Week 4	
Monday	4.5 Mile Run Perform 3-4 sets of each movement in the order provided 6 reps per movement Front Squat Dead Lift Hang Clean and Press Kettle Bell Swing Pull Up Power Clean Bench Press
Tuesday	35 Minutes Swimming 45 Pull Ups 70 Squats 125 Press Ups 220 Sit Ups
Wednesday	Perform 3-4 sets of each movement in the order provided 6 reps per movement Front Squat

| | Dead Lift
Hang Clean and Press
Kettle Bell Swing
Pull Up
Power Clean
Bench Press |
|---|---|
| Thursday | 1 Hour running steady state 70 intensity at incline 2-3% if doing it on treadmill

Sprints 6-8x100 M 25lb weight vest 30 seconds rest between sprints |
| Friday | Perform 3-4 sets of each movement in the order provided 6 reps per set
Front Squat
Dead Lift
Hang Clean and Press
Kettle Bell Swing
Pull Up
Power Clean
Bench Press |
| Saturday | Rest |
| Sunday | 3 Hours pack marching with 55lb pack |

Week 5	
Monday	5 Mile Run

Perform 3-4 sets of each movement in the order provided 12 reps per movement
Front Squat
Dead Lift
Hang Clean and Press
Kettle Bell Swing
Pull Up
Power Clean |

	Bench Press
Tuesday	40 Minutes Swimming 50 Pull Ups 80 Squats 135 Press Ups 230 Sit Ups
Wednesday	Perform 3-4 sets of each movement in the order provided 12 reps per movement Front Squat Dead Lift Hang Clean and Press Kettle Bell Swing Pull Up Power Clean Bench Press
Thursday	1 Hour running steady state 70 intensity at incline 2-3% if doing it on treadmill Sprints 4x150 M 35lb weight vest 45 seconds rest between sprints
Friday	Perform 3-4 sets of each movement in the order provided 12 reps per set Front Squat Dead Lift Hang Clean and Press Kettle Bell Swing Pull Up Power Clean Bench Press
Saturday	Rest
Sunday	3 Hours 30 Minutes pack marching with 55lb pack

Week 6	

Monday	5.5 Mile Run Perform 3-4 sets of each movement in the order provided 10 reps per movement Front Squat Dead Lift Hang Clean and Press Kettle Bell Swing Pull Up Power Clean Bench Press
Tuesday	45 Minutes Swimming 60 Pull Ups 100 Squats 150 Press Ups 250 Sit Ups
Wednesday	Perform 3-4 sets of each movement in the order provided 10 reps per movement Front Squat Dead Lift Hang Clean and Press Kettle Bell Swing Pull Up Power Clean Bench Press
Thursday	1 Hour running steady state 70 intensity at incline 2-3% if doing it on treadmill Sprints 6x150 M 35lb weight vest 45 seconds rest between sprints
Friday	Perform 3-4 sets of each movement in the order provided 10 reps per set Front Squat Dead Lift Hang Clean and Press Kettle Bell Swing Pull Up

	Power Clean
	Bench Press
Saturday	Rest
Sunday	3 Hours 30 Minutes pack marching with 55lb pack

Week 7	
Monday	6 Mile Run
	Perform 3-4 sets of each movement in the order provided 8 reps per movement
	Front Squat
	Dead Lift
	Hang Clean and Press
	Kettle Bell Swing
	Pull Up
	Power Clean
	Bench Press
Tuesday	40 Minutes Swimming
	65 Pull Ups
	120 Squats
	170 Press Ups
	270 Sit Ups
Wednesday	Perform 3-4 sets of each movement in the order provided 8 reps per movement
	Front Squat
	Dead Lift
	Hang Clean and Press
	Kettle Bell Swing
	Pull Up
	Power Clean
	Bench Press
Thursday	1 Hour running steady state 70 intensity at incline 2-3% if doing it on treadmill

	Sprints 8x150 M 35lb weight vest 45 seconds rest between sprints
Friday	Perform 3-4 sets of each movement in the order provided 8 reps per set Front Squat Dead Lift Hang Clean and Press Kettle Bell Swing Pull Up Power Clean Bench Press
Saturday	Rest
Sunday	3 Hours 30 Minutes pack marching with 55lb pack

Week 8	
Monday	6.5 Mile Run Perform 3-4 sets of each movement in the order provided 6 reps per movement Front Squat Dead Lift Hang Clean and Press Kettle Bell Swing Pull Up Power Clean Bench Press
Tuesday	45 Minutes Swimming 70 Pull Ups 140 Squats 185 Press Ups 285 Sit Ups
Wednesday	Perform 3-4 sets of each movement in the order provided 6 reps per movement Front Squat

	Dead Lift Hang Clean and Press Kettle Bell Swing Pull Up Power Clean Bench Press
Thursday	1 Hour running steady state 70 intensity at incline 2-3% if doing it on treadmill Sprints 10x150 M 35lb weight vest 45 seconds rest between sprints
Friday	Perform 3-4 sets of each movement in the order provided 6 reps per set Front Squat Dead Lift Hang Clean and Press Kettle Bell Swing Pull Up Power Clean Bench Press
Saturday	Rest
Sunday	3 Hours 30 Minutes pack marching with 55lb pack

Week 9	
Monday	7 Mile Run Perform 3-4 sets of each movement in the order provided 12 reps per movement Front Squat Dead Lift Hang Clean and Press Kettle Bell Swing Pull Up Power Clean

	Bench Press
Tuesday	50 Minutes Swimming 75 Pull Ups 160 Squats 200 Press Ups 300 Sit Ups
Wednesday	Perform 3-4 sets of each movement in the order provided 12 reps per movement Front Squat Dead Lift Hang Clean and Press Kettle Bell Swing Pull Up Power Clean Bench Press
Thursday	1 Hour running steady state 70 intensity at incline 2-3% if doing it on treadmill Runs 4x200 M 45lb weight vest 45 seconds rest between sprints
Friday	Perform 3-4 sets of each movement in the order provided 12 reps per set Front Squat Dead Lift Hang Clean and Press Kettle Bell Swing Pull Up Power Clean Bench Press
Saturday	Rest
Sunday	3 Hours 30 Minutes pack marching with 55lb pack

Week 10	

Monday	8 Mile Run
	Perform 3-4 sets of each movement in the order provided 10 reps per movement
	Front Squat
	Dead Lift
	Hang Clean and Press
	Kettle Bell Swing
	Pull Up
	Power Clean
	Bench Press
Tuesday	55 Minutes Swimming
	80 Pull Ups
	180 Squats
	220 Press Ups
	325 Sit Ups
Wednesday	Perform 3-4 sets of each movement in the order provided 10 reps per movement
	Front Squat
	Dead Lift
	Hang Clean and Press
	Kettle Bell Swing
	Pull Up
	Power Clean
	Bench Press
Thursday	1 Hour running steady state 70 intensity at incline 2-3% if doing it on treadmill
	Runs 6x200 M 45lb weight vest 45 seconds rest between sprints
Friday	Perform 3-4 sets of each movement in the order provided 10 reps per set
	Front Squat
	Dead Lift
	Hang Clean and Press
	Kettle Bell Swing
	Pull Up

		Power Clean
		Bench Press
Saturday		Rest
Sunday		3 Hours 30 Minutes pack marching with 55lb pack

Week 11	
Monday	8.5 Mile Run Perform 3-4 sets of each movement in the order provided 8 reps per movement Front Squat Dead Lift Hang Clean and Press Kettle Bell Swing Pull Up Power Clean Bench Press
Tuesday	60 Minutes Swimming 85 Pull Ups 200 Squats 240 Press Ups 350 Sit Ups
Wednesday	Perform 3-4 sets of each movement in the order provided 8 reps per movement Front Squat Dead Lift Hang Clean and Press Kettle Bell Swing Pull Up Power Clean Bench Press
Thursday	1 Hour running steady state 70 intensity at incline 2-3% if doing it on treadmill

	Runs 8x200 M 45lb weight vest 45 seconds rest between sprints
Friday	Perform 3-4 sets of each movement in the order provided 8 reps per set Front Squat Dead Lift Hang Clean and Press Kettle Bell Swing Pull Up Power Clean Bench Press
Saturday	Rest
Sunday	3 Hours 30 Minutes pack marching with 55lb pack

Week 12 Endurance Test Week	
Monday	8 Mile Run Best effort
Tuesday	Rest
Wednesday	Rest
Thursday	8 Mile Endurance pack march to be completed in 1 hour 50 minutes 55lb pack
Friday	Rest
Saturday	Rest
Sunday	12.5 Mile Endurance Pack march to be completed within 3 hours 25 Minutes 55lb Pack

Thank you for purchasing your copy of this book. I hope you find these programs of use in preparing you for whatever you will be undertaking in your military service or even reaching your peak.

For more information you can visit www.pnorthfitness.com for fitness articles and blog posts.

Printed in Great Britain
by Amazon.co.uk, Ltd.,
Marston Gate.